OLD RUSTIC

Tia meets a new friend

OLD RUSTIC

Rural Ruminations from Herefordshire

A collection of the monthly articles
which first appeared in the *Colwall Clock*

VOLUME II

John Bishop

Old Rustic: Rural Ruminations from Herefordshire
Volume Two
John Bishop

Published by Aspect Design 2014
Malvern, Worcestershire, United Kingdom.

Designed and Printed by Aspect Design
89 Newtown Road, Malvern, Worcs. WR14 1PD
United Kingdom
Tel: 01684 561567
E-mail: allan@aspect-design.net
Website: www.aspect-design.net

A copy of this book has been deposited with the British Library Board

ISBN 978-1-908832-61-0

CONTENTS

Padre and Bish taking communion!

INTRODUCTION

At long last, volume two of *Old Rustic.* Once again I would like to thank all my friends and wonderful characters who have been a large part of my life and who have contributed to the contents of this book. My particular thanks go to Padre for his help in getting volume two off the ground. As time goes by it appears that Padre and myself both share the same spiritual needs. Cheers mate!

I would also like to thank my old mate Cookie for his amazing cartoons. And, last but not least, my wife, Di, for her fantastic editing skills, making volume two possible, so I think it only right to dedicate this volume to her.

All proceeds of this book will be split between the Church Ale House Fund and the Ben Bathurst Memorial Trust, which supports a local military charity. The Memorial Trust is run and managed by the late Major's son, George Hervey-Bathurst.

Cookie

THEY FORECAST RAIN TOMORROW!

Nobody was more surprised than me at the response we had at the launch of the *Old Rustic* book on 18 February at the Park Hotel. It was a resounding success. I suppose, if I'm honest, I was slightly nervous about the occasion but once we had settled down and I was under the influence of a couple of gin and tonics (purely for medicinal purposes I hasten to add) the whole thing ran like clockwork. We managed to sell ninety-five books on the launch day. I was absolutely astonished at the book's popularity, and in fact by the end of February we had sold three hundred books in total, which will be a great boost to St James Church and Help for Heroes. None of this would have been possible without my editor, Di, who corrects my spelling mistakes, adds the odd punctuation mark and creates paragraphs here and there. I am still inclined to start my articles with a capital letter and eight hundred words later finish with a full stop. I would also take this opportunity to thank my good friend Padre who was the driving force behind the book. His wife, Sally, provided some lovely artwork and this, along with the cartoons created by Cookie, helped to bring the book alive.

So, we move on. This is not a time to rest on ones laurels. As most of you will be aware I have been voicing concerns about the lack of rainfall. Well, now it's official. The BBC has suddenly woken up to the fact that there is a problem! However, I do wish they would stop referring to the great drought of 1976 as there is no comparison with our current situation. Despite tremendously high temperatures in 1976, that drought actually finished on August Bank Holiday when the heavens opened and we had one of the wettest winters on record. Some misguided soul on TV this week suggested that we should give up eating meat and become vegetarians as animals drink a lot of water. What a silly statement, do people really think that plant life will still thrive in a drought—somehow I don't think so! Besides, can you imagine what a sad place the countryside would be without livestock? The worrying thing was that the TV presenter thought it was a good idea. Oh dear, what a sad state of affairs.

Anyway, never mind the drought. Neil, or Oscar as many of you will know him, has been wearing waterproofs all winter just in case a sudden deluge does hit us. In fact I think Neil wins the prize for quote of the month. When I asked him why he was wearing waterproofs with the temperature at 17° he said ' Well, they forecast rain tomorrow'! As you are probably aware, a new virus has appeared from Germany. It appears to be spread by midges and is called Schmallenberg disease. It causes congenital abnormalities in lambs. I would be lying if I said we are not concerned but you have to be positive and hope for the best and as I have said many times before, a sheep has one aim in life and that is to find a new way of dying. So at this stage we are all keeping our fingers crossed. We have faced disease problems before and this is just another hurdle to overcome.

But it's not all bad. The dry conditions are ideal for lambing, as wet weather is one thing that young lambs cannot cope with and I think it would be right to end on a positive note. Our first batch of ewes has lambed well. We have had our problems but no more than usual so, on we go, only another eight hundred to go.

STINKING BISHOP

You may or may not be aware that there is a direct link between myself and the now famous Stinking Bishop cheese. Stinking Bishop cheese rose to international prominence in 2005 when it featured in the Wallace and Gromit animation film *The Curse of the Were-Rabbit*. Despite its name and smell, the cheese is quite delicious. To create the aromatic flavour, the rind is washed in perry and stored in humid conditions. This creates the sweaty-sock aroma.

The perry used in the process is extracted from the Moorcroft pear—a local variety, probably propagated at Moorcroft farm at the edge of Colwall village. In common with many varieties, the Moorcroft pear goes by several names, depending on where it is grown. In Worcester it is known as Malvern Hills or Malvern Pear and in Colwall and Dymock the variety is known as Stinking Bishop.

My old friend Charles Martell began making Stinking Bishop cheese in 1994 from his herd of Gloucester cattle. His reason was to increase awareness of the breed which had been near extinction. The pear took its name locally from my great grandfather, Frederick Bishop, born in Pencome near Bromyard in the late nineteenth century. It was stated by my grandfather that the old boy had a stinking temper and was rather partial to the odd tipple. I know for a fact that once, after returning from the pub, he put the kettle on the stove to boil and when it wouldn't boil fast enough, he shot it! On another occasion, he sold a cow for seventeen pounds and ten shillings and didn't return from Ledbury until he had drunk the proceeds of the sale—some feat in the early 1900s.

My family produced a much celebrated perry from their pears and according to legend, the product cut you off at the knees, although it was stated that it was very easy to drink. The only problem was: it stopped your legs from functioning.

I feel very proud of this part of my family history. I love the old stories, the old characters, because after all, they are a huge part of our cultural heritage. Although it's frowned upon in some quarters, drinking is still enjoyed at Lavenger Bank, but now it's enjoyed for medicinal purposes; to lubricate the legs and not to render them useless!

A TRIP DOWN MEMORY LANE

On a recent trip to the Chase pub in Upper Colwall for rehydration therapy I decided to return home via Evendine Lane. The trip jogged my memory. I remembered driving my late grandfather in 1968 along exactly the same route and I can still remember some of the tales he shared with me over forty years ago. Grandfather told me he had grazed a large flock of sheep on the Malverns when he lived at Sally Beds in Evendine Lane, along with my Grandmother and their six children. According to grandfather our family had lived in most of the houses in Evendine Lane during the last century so it's not surprising that I have a real soft spot for its twisting lane and extremely picturesque views.

On our trip down what I suppose you could call memory lane, grandfather bombarded me with tales of the past. As we drove past the Kettle Sings he pointed out Gardiners Quarry, a business that was owned and run by Major Gardiner. Major was actually his Christian name, he was not a military man as far as I am aware. He was a tough old character who had actually travelled to Australia to help with the construction of railways under the guidance of one of the famous Ballard family. Grandfather had very clear memories of how he had helped with the installation of a steam boiler used to drive the stone crusher and he appeared to blame the installation process for a back injury that plagued him for most of his working life. As we drove past Perry Croft, where my father first started work at the age of thirteen, he asked me to pull over at the side of the road as he wished to show me a cross that had been cut into the roadside embankment. The cross had been cut into the embankment by a roadman to mark the spot where a local resident, Beverly Bowers, was killed. Beverly had run down off the hill and had been hit by a car and tragically died. We tried to find the cross but it seemed to have disappeared, probably grown over. I can just remember Beverly's sister, who lived on Colwall Green. Her name was Bess and she was married to Dickie Gwatkin, who worked at Colwall Station. They had named their house Beverly, presumably after her late brother. As grandfather and I turned down Evendine Lane we discussed Sir Barry Jackson the playwright. Sir Barry had lived at Black Hill until the late fifties when he built a new house, which he called Hambelton. He once asked my late father what you would say to a cow when it wouldn't stand still for milking. Father replied, 'Stand still you b—y thing!'

Sir Barry chuckled and replied, 'I can't write that into a play for the Birmingham Repertory Company!'

Our journey then took us down Evendine Lane and when we reached the first house on the right, which is at the top of Hawkins Pitch (the steep bit at the top of Evendine Lane) we stopped and discussed the gate that used to be part of the sheep pen at that location. Evidently most of the farmers with sheep on the hills had clubbed together to purchase the gate that closed off the road. Dad said it was commonplace to gather the sheep off the hills on a Sunday morning, closing the gate to create a pen. This would have the effect of closing the road to work on the flock. He said it was very rare to have to open the gate to let a vehicle through. Can you imagine the hue and cry if this same procedure was carried out today?

My grandfather's generation had lived through two world wars and had vivid memories of real hardship. At one stage he had run out of money and with no state handouts, unlike today, he went in search of employment in the coal pits of South Wales and actually got a job at Dowlas, a very tough place to survive in those days. Grandfather told me that one particular character had walked from Colwall to Manchester in search of employment and when the work dried up there he had walked to Southampton to search for another job. This poor soul actually walked along the Jubilee Drive en route to his next destination but didn't visit his family in the village because he was in such a dishevelled state. I can recall many more stories in relation to my trip down Evendine or Memory Lane, but there's just too much for one article.

Meanwhile, by the time you read this month's offering we will have launched the *Old Rustic* book, a compilation of stories about my memories of Cummins Farm and Colwall village life. The proceeds of the book will be going to St James Church, Colwall and Help for Heroes, both very worthy causes.

VINTAGE RUSTIC

Very few of you will be aware that my hobby is collecting and restoring classic vehicles and I suppose it would be right to say that I was bitten by the bug some twenty years ago when I purchased my first lorry from Freda Ballard. I approached Freda after the very untimely death of her late father, Charles Ballard. Charles had owned a 1938 Latil timber tractor, quite a rare machine in itself. Latil lorries originated in France but were built under licence in this country by a company called Chevoke & Drewry, famous for building dust carts. The Latils are rather strange vehicles, having four wheel steer and four wheel drive, which makes driving on the highway feel like sitting on a crab. The restoration of this vehicle took almost five years and was only made possible with the help of my old friend Simon Williamson. When we had finished Latil One I purchased a second Latil, an altogether much bigger and more powerful lorry. The same English company that built my first one built this one in 1948. Both lorries had spent all of their working lives in the timber industry, winching huge trees out of the woods and onto the timber trailers for transportation to the saw mills. Following the restoration of these two vehicles I took a breathing space for some five years until I decided to restore my late grandfather's grey Ferguson T20 tractor. This in itself was a very pleasing project as I can remember the little tractor arriving new at Cummins Farm in 1956. In fact it was the first tractor that I learned to drive in my early years. Harry Ferguson's little tractor completely transformed British agriculture during the post war years. The tractor had what was then a very advanced hydraulic system to attach and carry a range of implements specifically made for the machine. This was probably the only time that a complete range of implements had been designed and built around a tractor. So, as I have already said it was a great pleasure to restore granddad's pride and joy and it brought back many happy memories of the past, when life seemed to be moving at a less hectic pace.

The Rustic collection doesn't end there. Approximately five years ago Allan Lloyd and myself set sail for Sussex where we had located a totally unique Douglas lorry, which was in quite a sorry state with a broken axle and many other defects. Douglas manufactured lorries at Arle Road in Cheltenham for many years and this particular vehicle was built as a one off for British Rail and had actually spent all of its working life in and around Lowestoft. The Douglas lorry will probably be my last full restoration project and although I have spent hundreds of hours working on all of my vehicles there is a great sense of achievement and I'm very proud of my collection.

During August of this year I took off with three of my chums to a classic car auction. The four of us make up a good team: Allan Lloyd, also known as BP, is my technical advisor; Brian Lewis, who has been in the car trade all his life and is brilliant at picking up on any mechanical defects; and my old friend Roger Allsop who is my financial advisor (he will enjoy that title!). Anyway, to cut a long story short, I managed to purchase a 1925 Riley Tourer. The vehicle was built in Coventry and only thirty-six have survived to date. It comes from a period when motoring was much more sedate and leisurely, completely different from today's rat race. It's also a joy to drive as long as you're not in a hurry. When the Riley was first produced it was taken on a little test drive, not very far, just across the water, in fact to Nairobi. Can you imagine what sort of excursion that would have been and all without the aid of a sat nav?

I am sorry to have moved away from country matters in this

article but my vehicles are very much a part of my life. Also part of my life are my two step daughters, Alicia and Beth. Both girls have worked extremely hard and with Alicia now away at Manchester University studying Biomedical Sciences the house has been very quiet, but at least I don't have to watch *Coronation Street* or *X-Factor* so it's not all bad. As for Beth, she also had an amazing set of GCSE and music exam results and she recently played her oboe alongside the English Symphony Orchestra at Hereford Cathedral. We are all very proud of the girls and wish them well in their chosen careers.

SHEEP AND WORCESTER CATHEDRAL

For those of you who read last month's offering, you will be aware that we took two sheep to the grounds of Worcester Cathedral to fulfil a wish of Rory Johnson, who was trying to re-enact an ancient charter granted to Kings' School by Henry VIII. It was a great challenge but it soon became obvious that King Henry never had Trading Standards or Defra to deal with! It took approximately ten days for Trading Standards to get on the case . . . you see it appears that I went armed with the wrong licence—an absolutely heinous crime in their eyes, with the possibility of spreading plague and pestilence throughout the county. So, yours truly had to go cap in hand to the duty vet at Worcester to beg forgiveness and to ask him to grant the appropriate licence. I must say he was extremely helpful. I know it appears to have been somewhat of a storm in a teacup but it could have been very costly to me, with a fine well in excess of anything handed out for a first offence of dealing in cannabis! The fact that we had two sheep on a lawn outside of Worcester Cathedral, where it was unlikely that any bovine animals had grazed for a hundred years, had no bearing on the situation. It is rather bizarre that people can travel through countries where foot and mouth is endemic and then travel back to this country to walk through livestock markets without any form of bio security measures. So what started out as a bit of harmless fun nearly turned into a financial disaster!

It now appears that mindless bureaucracy is running out of control in British Agriculture and many other businesses, and singularly is the biggest threat to food production in this country. It has been stated that there are more Defra operatives than working farmers or drones (non-workers) as my late Uncle Walter called them—a very sad state of affairs.

At least one job was undertaken during May and June without the interference of Defra. I received a phone call from the Chairman of Pencome Parish Council. Pencome happens to be where my family originated during the early 1800s and, because of my interest in genealogy, I had studied the various gravestones in the cemetery and had in fact had a very interesting meeting with the local Rector. I had asked him to contact me if there were any problems with the ancient headstones of the family, and sure enough Health and Safety had visited the site and decided that Great Uncle Edwin's headstone was unsafe. Great Uncle Edwin had died in 1926. Although I was very grateful to the Chairman of the Council for informing me of the problem, I firmly believe that Health and Safety guidance in this respect should be questioned, as here they were suggesting that the headstone might fall on children in the churchyard. Well, first and foremost, children should not be allowed to play in the churchyard, as it is a place where you show respect and a place for quiet reflection, not an obstacle course. That also applies to the memorial garden, the most sacred of places. Anyway, on the first trip to Pencome a survey was carried out, headed by my good friend Roger Allsop, along with Carl Attwood (Padre) and myself. This was followed by a stop-over at the Green Dragon to draw up a plan of action. A week later the plan was hatched. Roger became Director of Operations, I was the labourer and Stuart Holland, or Toffee, as we know him, became our Health and Safety Officer, a very important role! After four trips to the churchyard, Great Uncle Edwin's headstone is now back to its original position and the Green Dragon has had its till topped up a number of times! As you can imagine, the whole procedure resembled a sketch from Last of the Summer Wine. I am very glad that Pencome Parish Council went to trouble of locating me. Maybe other Councils and Church supervisors should take a leaf out of their book and contact any known family members before demolishing memorials.

Anyway, back to Cummins Farm. Shearing took place in early June with three contract shearers spending three days with us. It's a dirty job and they really do earn their money. They charge £1.15 per sheep, but it's a real lost earner for me as a fleece is currently only valued at eighty pence—a very, very sad state of affairs, but there is no alternative as we only have one real outlet for the product. It is hard to imagine that so much wealth was created in the middle ages from the sale of wool and wool products, leading to the creation of so many of our great churches in Suffolk and the Cotswolds.

LET COMMON SENSE PREVAIL

Have you noticed that the media has suddenly woken up to the fact that a food crisis could be looming within twenty years? It's a fact that comes as no surprise to many of my farming colleagues. It has already been stated that the world population will hit nine-point-two billion by the year 2050 and with countries like China and India becoming more prosperous it's obvious that they will be sourcing food from all over the world to supplement their rather poor dietary arrangements. Many of us can remember the famous grain mountains of the sixties and seventies and also the so-called giant wine lake, but where has it all gone? Well, I have done my best to lower the wine lake over the past twenty years but the grain mountain has disappeared, almost certainly never to be seen again.

As a farmer, I would like to think that most of us who live in the countryside realise that the production of food is not as straightforward as the media would lead us to believe and it's no good thinking that the supermarkets will provide if the producer cannot produce. It never ceases to amaze me how the BBC can predict a bumper grain harvest in June or July, when the grain is rarely in the barn until September, and a wet August could have catastrophic consequences with large quantities of corn rotting in the fields, never to be harvested.

Over the last forty years there have been some tremendous changes in agriculture, not all good and definitely not all bad, but the pressure being placed on farmers not to produce food is at an all time high with the main emphasis now being on conservation measures. I even get paid for not clearing up fallen branches from trees to help the beetle population! Now, let me make it quite clear, I am not against conservation measures, far from it. On Cummins Farm we actually grow crops to feed wild birds. We also leave two metre margins around all the arable fields to help sustain wildlife, something that was quite unheard of in my father's day. As I see agriculture in the twenty-first century I see an industry that is being encouraged not to produce food, an industry that is being strangled by endless red tape and manipulated by extremely vociferous minority pressure groups, most of them totally detached from reality. I wonder if they would be so noisy if they were standing in long food queues. I know that many of you will think that this article is slightly over the top, but I can assure you that there has been very little encouragement from Westminster and even less from Brussels for farmers to get on and produce food. In fact one of our previous Ministers of Agriculture actually stated there was no need to produce food in this country as we could always import it!

LAMBING

Since I last put pen to paper for the Colwall Clock lambing has been in full swing at both Cummins Farm and Lavenger Bank, with well over a thousand lambs being born during March and although we have had our mishaps, on the whole the job has gone remarkably well. I know that many of you follow the Old Rustic column and will probably remember me saying that the writing was on the wall for an early spring—one of those statements you feel will come back to haunt you—but it couldn't have been further from the truth. March was brilliant for lambing with very little frost and practically no rain, an ideal situation for the main lambing period. In fact, a shortage of rain is quite a worry as one of the streams from Hope End has almost dried up. The lambing season is obviously a very hard slog. We've been working long hours, seven days a week for almost three months and we haven't been able to switch off from the job. It's played havoc with our social life and it hasn't given me much of a chance to support the village pubs either! I cannot over-emphasise the help and support that Diane has given. She has taken over the night shifts in the 'maternity ward' allowing me to get to bed reasonably early so that I can make an early start in the morning. I think the earliest I managed to get going was three o'clock, an unearthly time of day by any standards. Di didn't come from a farming background but she has taken to shepherding like a duck to water, she just rolls up her sleeves and gets on with it. The other person who has been of great assistance to us is Johnny Davies. We managed to coax John out of retirement and believe it or not he seemed to be enjoying every minute of it! He even managed to handle Neil and that's not an easy task! John's wife, Alison, appeared on a number of occasions and helped with the water carrying to all the individual pens, a laborious task as we have over sixty pens of thirsty sheep which need watering at least three times a day. Lambing is a great challenge to any farmer, you are working with an animal that has a life-long ambition to find a new way of dying but it's a great feeling to see the lambs frolicking through the daffodils and playing with their mates when their mothers' backs are turned.

You may have noticed in passing that a few things have changed at Cummins Farm. The sheep flock is expanding at the expense of the cattle herd because, after much deliberation and soul searching, we have decided to give up our small beef-fattening unit. A number of reasons brought this decision to a head and quite honestly I feel rather sad about it as there have been cattle on Cummins Farm since grandfather took over the holding in 1933. But due to the ongoing debacle over tuberculosis we have decided to leave the beef cattle alone. TB is not a subject that I wish to be drawn into but something has to be done to control this terrible disease. It's not fair on the livestock or on the farmers and as usual nobody wants to grasp the nettle and try to come up with a solution. So, until we get some accurate guidance from both government and Defra there will be no more beef fattened at Cummins Farm.

FOOD FOR THOUGHT

I have been writing articles for the Colwall Clock for almost four years. I have rarely cheated by stealing someone else's comments and, as most of you will realise, my stories are about my own personal experiences or that of my family. However, for this months offering I would like to cheat a little. My old friend, Allan Lloyd, has recently lent me a book. Allan said, 'You will enjoy this, it's right up your street.' In fact it's written by A. G. Street—please excuse the pun! The book is called *Farming England*, published in 1936 and it provides an insight into agriculture since 1820, right through to its year of publication. The reason I have chosen to cheat a little is because I think there is a parallel to what is happening today both in agriculture and the countryside. In 1820, country folk outnumbered towns' folk. Thirty years later they were on a fifty–fifty basis. Sixty years later it had fallen even further, to 22 per cent of rural dwellers and by 1936 just 13 per cent of the population remained in the countryside.

For the last fifty years the number of people living in the countryside has steadily increased. That said, there has been a dramatic decrease in people involved solely in agriculture or food production, as we know it, due to mechanisation. Of course seasonal workers in the soft fruit industry boost this number during the summer months.

Since 1931 our farming acres have been shrinking by at least

31,000 acres per annum, especially in the southeast and I would go even further than that by saying that motorways and business parks are consuming valuable land at a far greater rate than those figures. There are many home truths in this article, which are relevant to what is happening today. Firstly, it is without doubt impossible for our town dwellers to feed themselves, yet this doesn't stop them from telling us how the countryside should be managed, with their emphasis being on recreation and not food production. Sentimentality concerning our countryside is rife and incorrect information even more so, mainly down to the fact that most of our generation have never experienced food shortage and have always taken it for granted that food will appear from somewhere in the world to end up in their beloved supermarkets.

Some time ago I was asked to speak on the *Jeremy Vine Show* on Radio Two to discuss weather conditions, which were affecting the transportation of food due to the serious snowfall we were experiencing. At the time there were serious concerns over transporting milk, cattle, sheep and vegetables from the farms. Yet, I followed a woman who was the editor of an urban-based magazine. She said it was impossible to have food shortages in the twenty-first century. It took me only a few words to put her right, but to be fair to her she was only voicing the beliefs and opinions of the urban masses.

We farmers are constantly criticised by ill-informed minority pressure groups that have forgotten that the majority of the countryside is a working environment and that amazing patchwork quilt that you see before you is because of us, not in spite of us. In summing up, I would say never take food production for granted, a sentiment that will be echoed by all gardeners and allotment holders, especially in the type of weather conditions we have just experienced. And let's not forget the vast quantities of wheat that are now being removed from the food chain for use in production of plastics and bio-fuels, which means that food and energy production is now on a collision course. I fear that there are interesting times ahead.

TRANSPORT

The one aspect of agriculture I have never touched on is the transportation of livestock. When my grandfather took over Cummins Farm in 1933 it was not unusual for my father and his brother Walter to walk sheep and cattle to Defford Common, a distance of some fifteen miles and it was also commonplace to drive their animals to Ledbury market, a feat that is unimaginable in today's world.

My late Uncle Walter was a great fountain of knowledge when it came to the movement of livestock and in many ways this article is dedicated to his memory. I spent many hours with Walter talking about the hardships of his early years during our travels to and from the markets, and also in latter years after his retirement when he resided at Evendine House. Walter said that in those days it was common practise to walk geese to market but before they set out on a journey the geese would be walked through soft tar and then fine gravel to form a wearing surface on their feet. I'm sure this story will sound far-fetched to many of you but there were very few lorries available to transport the animals at that time. He told me that when he was very young the old farmers had told him that hundreds of geese and poultry would be kept in a pound at Wynds Point overnight to be rested before they continued their journey towards the Midlands. Can you imagine the chaos if you tried to drive a few hundred geese up the A449 today?

One of Walter's favourite stories really sticks in my mind; he told me that on one occasion my grandfather had sheep at tack at Pontrilas (a system where you pay so much per week per head for the upkeep of the animals). In those days it was commonplace to move animals by train and when this particular flock was deemed fit they were duly sent to Hereford market by rail, only to find when they came up for auction they didn't even get a bid. So, without more ado grandfather said 'Well, we have no money so I suppose we'd better walk them back to Colwall!' They left Hereford in the afternoon and walked the sheep as far as Tarrington, where the sheep decided enough was enough and refused to walk any further. Grandfather arranged to leave them in an orchard overnight promising to return the following day to collect them. Now, you might think that this is the end of the story but it got worse for Walter and grandfather. They walked on to Ledbury Station where they missed the last train home and had to continue on foot to Colwall and the following morning had to turn round and walk all the way back to Tarrington to collect their flock.

As I've already stated it was quite normal to transport animals by train, as most stations had handling facilities where the stock could be loaded or unloaded at ease. Stock would then be transferred by road, very often by drovers, to neighbouring farms or markets. The drovers were a very special type of people; they would walk the animals from the markets either to and from farms or to abattoirs or local butcher's shops where very often the butcher had his own slaughtering facilities. According to Walter, two of the best drovers were Italian. One of them, whose name was Antonio, had a bad accident when he was run over by a car. He lost part of his leg so he retired from driving livestock and managed to pedal a tricycle, which doubled up as an ice cream cart, selling his wares at the British Camp car park. Can you imagine pedalling that contraption with just one leg?

According to Mrs Lloyd, on one occasion my father went to Barton Fair at Gloucester market with his friend John Hind, who farmed at Netherpath. The pair of them returned to Colwall with two rams on the train. I don't know whether the rams travelled first or second class!

I can just remember the cattle trains coming through Colwall in the mid-fifties loaded up with hundreds of animals, very often store cattle, which had come all the way from Ireland via Hollyhead. But, how things have changed. We now have huge lorries, which can transport 450 sheep and believe it or not, in less compact conditions than we have come to accept on London Underground!

As this is my first offering of the New Year, I wish you all a happy and peaceful 2011.

SHEEP JUDGING

As I mentioned in last month's article, sheep judging is in full swing at both Hereford and Hay on Wye markets. Once again my colleague, Dick Edwards, and myself were invited to Hay and Hereford to judge the annual ram shows. This proved to be a great challenge, mainly because of the number of animals coming forward and also the high quality of the sheep on offer making it very difficult for us to come to any easy decision. We always enjoy our trip to Hay on Wye, especially the drive down the Golden Valley via Peterchurch and this year was particularly enjoyable as Diane came along to the evening Ram Sale and actually got involved on the sidelines. One of the biggest problems with ram judging is that we have to contend with so many breeds, all having different attributes. For instance, Beltex sheep have tremendous muscle conformation but many of them lack overall length, whereas the traditional black-faced Suffolks have plenty of length but lack the muscle conformation of the continental breeds such as Texel and Charolais. Hay on Wye is a small market in comparison with Hereford but there is always a good atmosphere and a very competitive spirit amongst the mainly Welsh farmers. With nearly two hundred rams to chose from, the atmosphere became quite tense, especially in the continental class with four different breeds for us to judge. Diane didn't join us in the ring but I told her to write down the number of the animal that she considered to be best in show and low and behold she came up with the same animal as Dick and myself, quite a feat considering the quantity and quality of the animals on offer. When we had given out the prize cards the auction got underway and I must say that the bidding, which is still done in guineas, was extremely spirited with a lot of the better quality rams fetching 25 per cent more than last year's prices. I normally buy most of my rams at either Hay or Hereford market and this year we actually bought the first prize ram from Hay for a price well in excess of anything I have paid out in the past but with luck it will pay off with better progeny.

Anyway, moving on. By the time this article goes to press it will be November, probably my least favourite month. It's early winter, the days are short, the mud starts to get deep, the rain is usually cold and I have to scrape the ice off the windscreen in the mornings. Not only that, I know that there is a chance that we will have a hard winter and with feed prices going through the roof due to the cost of raw materials it could be a very expensive time for us. But looking back at last winter's disastrous weather in the early part of the year isn't it amazing how the plants burst into life when the temperature eventually began to warm up? I don't think I can remember such an amazing year for fruit of all types and although we are not directly involved in apple production, it is very pleasing to see all the local orchards bearing such a heavy crop. Not only has it been a good year for apples, but plums, damsons, cherries and pears have also been in abundance and last but not least we are expecting a wonderful harvest of sloes. This should come as good news for my friend Nick Neve, who was somewhat concerned about this year's crop . . . Well Nick, you come up with the gin and I'll come up with the sloes and if you're really lucky I might even help you sample some of the finished product!

WHAT A GAS

There was great excitement at the beginning of May when two of my friends asked if they could use their metal detectors on Lavenger Bank. They hadn't been out there long when they found a Roman coin. The coin was in remarkably good condition and was actually lying just beneath the surface. After some investigation we discovered that the coin came from the reign of the Emperor Victorius. It appears that Victorius only reigned for a very short space of time, from 267 AD to 271 AD. He was apparently rather a naughty boy—he was caught committing adultery and was subsequently stabbed to death by an irate husband! They found many other items including musket balls and a number of brass buckles but so far, unfortunately, no Saxon hoard.

On Cummins Farm, Simon and Joe Blandford have arrived to do the shearing. It's a dirty job but they seem to revel in it. We manage to shear approximately two hundred ewes a day so it takes us about five days to complete the flock. For many years the value of wool has been a disgrace and the operation has lost us money, but this year the price has doubled so we might see a small profit on the sale of the wool. As far as I can gather, the reason for the price increase is a buoyant export trade, plus the fact that wool is back in fashion and is also being used as insulation material in the construction industry.

How many times have you had to ring one of the utility companies and felt that you were banging your head against a brick wall? Well, I have just had one of those experiences. Many of you will be aware of the area known as Flapgate Lane and will be very aware that there is an old barn situated between Cummins Farm and Flapgate Cottage. Approximately a month ago the gas main that supplies Ledbury sprung a leak in one of our fields. The leak is so bad that you can actually feel the gas forcing its way through the soil. Anyway, without further ado I phoned the emergency number from the Yellow Pages and explained to the operator that a rather serious gas leak had occurred in an eighteen-acre field of oil seed rape. I explained that the field was in the heart of the countryside and that it was at least forty yards from the highway and that the nearest house was at least five hundred yards away. But all of this information was to no avail; the operator was obviously acting under the strict guidelines laid down by the gas supplier, so no matter what I said she was going to have her say too! This included telling me not to switch the light on or if I felt the need to close the door I must close it manually and not electronically and last but not least if the room

required ventilation I could open the window. It was at this stage I explained to her that I was rapidly losing the will to live and would try my best to persuade Neil, my employee, not to have one of his famous bonfires in the immediate area. So far, the gas has been escaping for a month, but we do have a sign in the lane asking us not to smoke and all this has taken longer than it took the Irish 'navvies' to dig the pipe in by hand across Cummins Farm in 1955 when we lived in Flapgate! But, I suppose, this is the price we pay for progress.

A LITTLE BIT OF ROMAN INFLUENCE

For those of you who follow Old Rustic on a regular basis, I feel sure you will remember the problem we were having with the gas board over a rather serious leak in my field of oilseed rape. Well the outcome was very much like the old Flanders and Swan ditty, which, if my memory serves me correctly, started 'it was on the Monday morning the gas man came to call' and it was a Monday when they exhumed the pipe! But, guess what, they didn't have the right clamp to seal the leak which came as no surprise to Neil and myself. And would you believe that by the following Monday it was hissing away merrily? So, I rang them up and told them I'd seen children playing with matches over the leak, which wasn't exactly true. But guess what, it was on the Tuesday morning the gas man came to call and this time he had the correct repair kit, now there's a surprise!

Do you get the feeling that this year has flown past much faster than last year? It seems only days since we finished lambing and yet here we are weaning the lambs and getting their mums ready to meet their boyfriends all over again. The lamb prices have been at an acceptable level this year with a very buoyant trade throughout the season. This is mainly due to a very strong export demand, although hiccups with the Euro have slightly depressed the market trend. Weather wise it's been a strange year. Firstly the grass and arable crops suffered from the shortage of rain and then the hay making proved quite difficult due to an onset of localised storms which made it a very stop–go affair. But without doubt we actually got lucky for once, and I don't think we made one bad bale. During July the crops bulked up quite well, enabling us to replenish our very depleted winter fodder stocks. It never ceases to amaze me how mechanisation has taken over agriculture; this year in particular every bale produced on Cummins Farm was handled mechanically. In fact, from 24 to 27 July we baled and hauled twenty acres of hay and harvested thirty-four acres of winter barley and thirty-five acres of oilseed rape. The barley hardly touched down in the store before lorries appeared and the whole crop was taken to Avonmouth to be shipped off to Egypt.

A few months ago two of my friends came to Lavenger Bank with their metal detectors and in fact, as I have already stated in a previous article, they managed to find a Roman coin dating from the time of Emperor Victorus. Well finds have steadily continued to grow; so far they have found musket balls, four George III halfpennies, two George III cartwheel pennies, another badly worn Roman coin, a William III shilling dating from 1690, a Roman broach from the first century AD, a small pendant and two silver rings which appeared to be quite modern. But their best find to date happened in Colwall churchyard; as many of you will be aware, my old friend Alec Hutton passed away on 30 June. Alec's wife Lesley and her family joined a full congregation for a thanksgiving service, and afterwards we took tea and cake outside the Ale House. It was while we were there that Alec's son Andrew realised he'd lost a signet ring given to him by his late father on his twenty-first birthday. Andrew contacted me and I arranged for my metal detecting friends to search the area, and after seven hours they had a result and returned the ring to it's very grateful owner.

Meanwhile, Hereford market has moved to a new site on the outskirts of the town, just off the Roman Road. I've been assured by the auctioneers that the new market would not have been built if it hadn't have been for an ancient charter granted by Elizabeth I in 1597, so no matter what our councillors or politicians say, the truth is that if the charter had not been granted, the new market would not exist today.

And, finally, isn't it nice to see the Waller family making a success of the butchers shop in our village? We're hoping to see a return of local Colwall lamb in the very near future so watch this space!

THE ROYAL FAMILY IN COLWALL

Well at long last the rains have arrived after what has been the driest winter on record. It now appears we have just endured the wettest April since records began. The stream from Hope End turned into a raging torrent overnight and the whole situation has become quite bizarre. Now I know that you will say he's a typical farmer, never satisfied, always complaining, but this amount of rain at this time of the year makes life on the farm very difficult. It's almost impossible to work on the sheep due to the muddy conditions and so routine worming of the flock gets put back adding to increased health problems and, in some more severe cases, can even lead to death. Not only is it a problem with livestock husbandry, but also crop spraying is totally out of the question so the weeds are now growing out of control.

On Friday 13 April I heard the cuckoo for the first time, and I have to say I almost felt sorry for him. I was walking round a bunch of ewes and lambs at six o'clock in the morning with ice on my boots at the time and the poor bird sounded as if he had laryngitis, which wasn't surprising given the temperature. Then, within days of hearing the cuckoo we were moving the sheep off the same field as it had become seriously waterlogged.

Let's hope the weather brightens up for the Queen's Diamond Jubilee before celebrations begin in earnest. I can remember celebrating the Queen's visit to Colwall in 1957. I was a pupil at Colwall Infant School and we all walked up Evendine Lane and sat on the lower slopes of the Herefordshire Beacon, just above the Camp car park. We were all equipped with our Union Jack flags and sat quietly awaiting the arrival of the Royal entourage. After some delay the Queen and the Duke of Edinburgh arrived at the British Camp. We found out later that the procession had been held up by a flock of sheep that had strayed onto the highway, and just for once these sheep were not mine. If my memory serves me correctly, Roy Rowlands, who lived at Brand Lodge, was the High Sherriff at the time. He was there to greet

the Royal couple and as he approached them he managed to trip over his ceremonial sword! This raised quite a laugh amongst me and my school chums. It was a marvellous occasion enjoyed by all but I must admit it was a long walk back to the school on Colwall Green; after all I was only seven years of age.

The next time we were treated to a Royal visit was in 1960 when the late Queen Mother visited Bush Farm to take tea with Lord Cilcennin, who was the current Lord Lieutenant of

Herefordshire. The Royal car arrived at its destination via the Old Colwall Road. We were a small group standing at the junction near to what is now my home and it was was very exciting to receive a royal wave from the Queen Mother. It was another very special occasion and something I will never forget. Incidentally, it was stated that prior to the Royal visit to Bush Farm, the village handyman, Len Bourne, was summoned to paint the bathroom, just in case Her Majesty required the facilities!

As for the Diamond Jubilee, I feel sure that most of us will celebrate in our own special way. Di and myself, along with many others, will be attending a dinner party at the Park Hotel where we will raise a glass or two to the Royal couple and I for one think they thoroughly deserve it.

THE ROYAL WEDDING

April's weather has been incredible with long dry periods and mainly frost-free nights, making our job so much easier, but everything has a down side and we are beginning to get desperate for rain. The stream that runs from the lake at Hope End has completely dried up and the top of the banks, where the topsoil is shallow, has started to burn up, a situation that is almost unheard of during the month of April. But, as I have said before, nature has a way of redressing the balance so I suppose when it does start to rain it won't know when to stop!

The month seems to have flown by and, with lambing over and most of the land-work finished, we decided to take a day off to celebrate the Royal Wedding and what a day it turned out to be. On the great day, I started work extra early as I always go round my sheep first thing. We have nine bunches, which take about two hours to get round, but one of the bunches at Flapgate had been visited the night before so I decided not to stop there and drove straight past onto my next destination. When I reached the next field of sheep I realised that my youngest dog, Jack, had disappeared off the face of the earth, so I backtracked to the farm and all the fields I'd visited on my rounds but there was no sign of him. I eventually discovered that Jack, being a keen working dog, had acted on instinct and decided to jump out of the truck at Flapgate to check out the sheep I'd missed earlier. Believe it or not he had rounded them up into the corner of the field and was sitting waiting for me to inspect them! So, panic over, it was time to get dressed up for the Royal occasion.

Mother in law had come to stay so I decided to earn some brownie points and book us all into the Park Hotel to enjoy the Wedding and what a fantastic time we had. Iain and Sarah Nesbitt were marvellous hosts, providing coffee and biscuits to start with and a sumptuous buffet lunch to follow, rounded off with a few glasses of bubbly to toast the Royal couple. I'm sure you'll agree that the wedding was an amazing spectacle with everything going like clockwork. We sat transfixed by the big screen. We might be a small country in stature but when it comes to pageantry we are head and shoulders above the rest of the world, others just don't come a close second. By the time we arrived home we were still on a high, full of stories about the great event. Was it the dress, the uniforms, the horses, the carriages, the fashion or the thousands of spectators that made it such a special day, or was it just that we all needed a bit of a lift that made us so pleased that it all went so well? The day didn't end there for us. Some friends arrived with a magnum of champagne so we toasted the happy couple again (and again) and sang the National Anthem then watched the replay—all over again!

DIAMOND JUBILEE

I am not ashamed to say that farming was definitely on the back burner during the weekend of the Diamond Jubilee. For us, it all began on Wednesday when my mother-in-law arrived from Durham. She is an ardent Royalist along with the rest of our family so celebrations got underway at Lavenger Bank long before the weekend.

For some six months Iain and Sarah Nesbitt, also great Royal supporters, had been planning a dinner combined with a fund-raising event for Help for Heroes at the Park Hotel. This took place on Friday 1 June and was a resounding success. Almost ninety people attended a sumptuous four-course dinner and with more than enough wine the party was off to a good start. When the meal drew to a close the speeches began and with my old friend Padre (aka Carl Attwood) as the Impresario the evening was obviously going to be a great success. We sang 'God Save the Queen', 'Jerusalem', 'Land of Hope and Glory' and a version of 'Bless this House', written by our Impresario, especially to capture the mood of the occasion. It went as follows:

Bless the Park O Lord we pray
Keep it solvent day by day
Bless John Bish that he may be
Potent 'til he's ninety three
Bless our forces Lord that they

Safe in our defence may stay
Bless our Queen that she may be
Blessed this year of Jubilee
Bless us all that we may be
Ever mindful Lord of thee

So as you can imagine everything was going very well. It was at this stage when yours truly was given the chance to say a few words and present our guest speaker, Mick Clifford OBE, with two cheques from sales of the *Old Rustic* book: one for £500 to the Clock Tower Appeal and one for £500 to the late Major Ben Bathurst fund with the money going directly to SAS widows. Mick was an RSM in the SAS and although he has recently retired from the regiment he is heavily involved in fund raising for Help for Heroes and the Clock Tower appeal (the SAS fund). He now has a small farm raising Highland Cattle and, along with his wife Sue, keeps the Crown and Anchor pub in Lugwardine where he sells his home produced steaks and I can assure you it is one of the finest pubs in Herefordshire. If you feel the need to make a visit, always say you know Bish and take my advice and order a T-bone.

After the presentation James Pugh conducted a very successful auction and with plenty of spirited bidding (in more ways than one) we eventually raised in the region of £8,000. At the end of the event there was a standing ovation. I think we should all feel justly proud of our achievements and I'm sure that Her Majesty would have approved.

Saturday turned into a day to reflect on a job well done or maybe as my late grandfather would have said, a case of 'joyful nights bring sorrowful days'! Celebrations continued on Sunday at Lavenger Bank with another sumptuous spread for a few of our close friends. This time I was in charge of the champagne, wine and port and after severe over-indulgence we watched the flotilla going down the Thames from the comfort of the armchair, a very sensible place to be considering the weather conditions. More celebrations took place on Monday night when we joined

Peter and Sharon Maiden at their beacon on Oyster Hill. It was a wonderful evening, very well supported and a great vantage spot to see many of the beacons being lit across Herefordshire. I would like to say a big thank you to Peter, Sharon and Alex for making such a fantastic effort on what turned out to be an extremely memorable evening.

Finally, we arrived at Tuesday. I was spotted en route to the Park Hotel driving my 1925 vintage Riley. I had just settled down to a quiet pint with Iain and Sarah Nesbitt when Nicky Carless accosted me and asked if I would head the procession from the Clock meadow to the Village Hall. This was a challenge too good to miss so four of us squeezed into the old car and set off at the front of the procession led by Mike Poulson proudly waving his Union Jack in front of us. A very small Spiderman who constantly flexed his muscles along the way followed us closely! I personally think Mike would have looked better waving a red flag as often happened in the early days of motoring but given the occasion we will let let him off!

So, five days of celebration drew to a close and I have to say I don't think there is another country in the world that can arrange a pageant like the Brits. We should all feel justly proud for playing a part in it, so God Bless the Queen, may she long reign over us.

THE WAR YEARS

This article covers the war years in Colwall and I would like to dedicate it to the memory of my mother who died on 22 December 2008. Although she was born in London and was in fact a milliner at Harvey Nichols she had joined the Women's Land Army working at Mill Farm for the duration of the war. She told me that she went from making hats for members of the Royal Family to pulling sugar beet in three days. Although work was hard, she enjoyed the peace and quiet having lived through the Blitz.

Agriculture went through its greatest changes, probably since the Enclosures Act, during the war years with a huge need to feed the population, as food could not be imported due to the constant threat to merchant shipping by German U-boats. With the introduction of a new piece of government legislation, known as War-Agg, life at Cummins Farm changed overnight. My family was instructed to plough most of the farmland to grow wheat, sugar beet and potatoes to feed the nation. Growing the crops was not a straightforward operation. Although grandfather had purchased his first tractor, there were huge problems with weed and pest control as there were very few chemicals available at the time. Father told me it was not uncommon to harvest less than 10 cwt to the acre whereas the same fields today would probably produce around three tons to the acre.

Although food production was the main aim at Cummins

Farm my father had joined the Home Guard (Dads Army!) and spent most nights on patrol. He told me he had spent many a night guarding the smoke vent next to the Ballard cemetery to try and prevent saboteurs from blowing up the tunnel. He was there the night Coventry was bombed and said he could clearly hear the explosions. The front meadow at Cummins Farm housed a searchlight and an anti-aircraft gun. There were dugouts on Lavenger Bank and an ammunitions store in a field adjacent to the Bartons Holloway and father was issued with solid shot for his twelve-bore shotgun. I think it was quite late in the war before the platoon was equipped with Lee Enfield 303 rifles but

they did practise throwing hand grenades. He said the first one that was thrown fell in a cow pat and they were all covered in something quite unmentionable!

Colwall was hit by a stick of bombs that exploded at Knell Farm killing some of the farmer's stock but there were no civilian casualties. We had a number of planes come down in the area, one was an American Mustang fighter which crashed in Hope End Park killing the pilot.

Although mechanisation had started to arrive on farms there was a great shortage of manpower. This was one of the reasons that the Women's Land Army was formed. Most of these girls came from the towns and cities but soon adapted to the farm way of life. There were a number of Italian prisoners working at the farm during those difficult times and in fact one of the few reminders we have of that time is written on a wall at Cummins Farm by a man called Vincenzo who clearly showed his dislike for both Hitler and Mussolini!

I say again how did we manage to feed a nation during those war years yet today's local food production is diminishing despite the growing concerns around our carbon footprint? We have a minister in charge who shows little regard for the human resources of British agriculture and cannot see how important agriculture is to the supply of food to this country.

I find it hard to close my latest offering, possibly because my late mother played such an integral part in Colwall's farming history in a time that has passed but will never be forgotten.

COLWALL PAST AND PRESENT

In last month's issue I touched on the fact that there were eight dairy herds in Colwall so I thought I would expand on that statement.

If my memory serves me correctly the following farms produced milk in the village: Bill Houlbrooke at Ockridge Farm, Phillip Archer at Netherpaths; Jeff Pedlingham at Lower House; Jack Harry at Upper Mill, who also had a small delivery round; Ernest Price at Mill Farm; William Sear at Park Farm; Mr Tadman at Moorcroft Farm and my grandfather at Cummins Farm. During this period most of the milk went into churns and was collected by Cadbury Brothers but we were the exception to the rule, bottling the milk we produced and supplying the village.

At that period there were many other small farms in the village. Eby Owen lived and farmed at Old Castle; he also farmed the racecourse. Uncle Walter farmed the Tan House and the Winnings and Uncle Jack had Lower Mill and some small fields in Evendine. Hoe Farm was in the hands of Mike Fitzer, Jeff Smithson farmed Brock Hill and Stan Hill farmed Redlands and land in Brockhill Road. There were numerous small holders including Arthur Hill, Mr Bousfield, Mr Nash, Charlie Pedlingham, Peter Preece, Mrs Barbour Simpson, Miss Mayhew who kept pedigree Ryland sheep and Mr Vernon Dent at Fortunes Gate who bred pedigree Suffolks. And, last but not least, Reg Wingate who kept pigs in Martin's Orchard. Both Moorcroft and the Bush were part of the Old Colwall estate and I believe were managed by the Holland Martin family from Overbury. Miss Parr ran a poultry unit at the Glebe House and also milked a couple of cows. Ron Hitchins had pigs and a few cattle, Alec Berry kept pigs at Mr Ballard's model piggery and Harry Pedlingham, known by most of us as 'Missed it' (though I'm not really sure why) milked a couple of cows and kept pigs, one of them being so prolific she actually got a mention in the Guinness Book of Records!

I must say that my list of farms has even surprised me and a rough calculation would suggest that somewhere between forty to fifty people were employed on the farms during the early 1960s—a tremendous contrast to today's numbers of approximately four farm workers and seven farmers.

I suppose in the interests of efficiency all the small units have been absorbed with huge dairy herds of three hundred cows being the norm, the milk being sent hundreds of miles before eventually ending up on your doorstep or on the supermarket shelf. Never mind, some folk call this progress but I'm not so sure. Having said that, I am as guilty as the dairy farmers, producing more lambs at Cummins Farm than probably the whole of Colwall did in 1960 and although we still manage to supply lambs to Paul Gurney in Ledbury, the bulk of the lambs end up on the supermarket shelves, travelling miles because of the lack of local abattoirs.

Talking of lambs brings me forward to this moment in time; lambing has started at Cummins and, although we now lamb inside, it's still very hard work with long hours and a huge reliance on reasonable weather for turning out the newborn lambs. I suppose it's a bit like a production line—you have to keep moving them outside in to the field or you create a log jam.

At this stage it would be remiss of me not to mention the passing of a dear old family friend and although many of you never met Noey Lewis he was one of the greatest characters Colwall ever produced. Noey was born at New Court (the old house). He started work with Mr Constable in Malvern Wells as an apprentice plumber and eventually went to work for Roland James, a well-known builder at Upper Colwall. He became a great authority on the water systems at Barton Court, Old Colwall and Schweppes, maintaining the supply with his old friend, Jack Greening. He joined the army in 1942 and had an amazing war record, joining the Royal Engineers and then the 6th Airborne, seeing action in many major battle zones of the Second World War. He returned to work for Mr James after the war and could always be seen wearing his famous red beret with pride and quite rightly so. I spent many happy hours with Noey and his late wife Dora (Nor) helping them to drink his homemade wine. We still have five gallons on tap; it's ten years old and has turned into the elixir of life! Noey recently passed away at the age of ninety-eight; a very good innings for a very close friend.

HOUDINI THE DERBYSHIRE GRITSTON EWE

When I was a child we always had pet sheep in the flock or 'tiddlers' as we called them. Most of them had started life as orphans and had been reared on the bottle, a practice that doesn't happen any more as today we prefer to use foster-mothers. If they were females there was always a good chance that they would join the breeding flock and although it was sometimes helpful to have a sheep that was almost domesticated it could also be a nuisance as they would defy the dogs and when you were feeding they were constantly around your feet, very often managing to trip you up leaving you face down in the mud, or in the worst case scenario, run between your legs and take off at a great rates of knots which had even more dire consequences. Then you have sheep that are the total opposite of tiddlers; they will not conform with any form of flock management and rarely stay in the same field as their mates and in many cases are almost unmanageable when you have to catch them for routine maintenance. But one ewe on Cummins Farm didn't fit into any of these categories. She became known as Houdini, obviously after the great escapologist. Not only was she good at escaping from any field we placed her in, she was also belligerent, determined, cantankerous and sometimes downright cheeky! I purchased Houdini as a two year old from Mrs Armitage about twelve years ago, which made her fourteen years old, a great age for a sheep. We soon realised that she was going to be a law unto herself.

When Houdini first arrived, it was quite obvious she was going to be a problem. We would place her in a field along with six hundred other ewes and if you had time to observe her you would see that she would walk round the perimeter, return to the gate and give you a look that said, 'I won't be here in the morning.' The strange thing was that although she was a great escapologist she was always easy to handle—if you could catch her—never kicking or struggling during worming, shearing or foot trimming, unlike some of her counterparts. As the years went by, she became a loner, living in the old parkland adjacent to Colwall Church but she would always find a boyfriend in the autumn and produce two fine lambs in the spring. During one particular winter she disappeared completely and although we searched high and low for her, both Neil and myself feared the worst. So it came as quite a shock when during April of the following year she appeared with two beautiful lambs with

similar habits to their mother, negotiating hedges and fences with ease and eventually settling in a wood near Wellington Heath where they grazed and grew until the following autumn until they were mature enough to break out into a neighbour's flock of ewes and do what comes naturally. I suppose time eventually caught up with the old girl. She gave the rams a miss for the last few years of her life and chose to spend her final years in the Park field by the Church, which she shared with Ron Smith's piebald ponies, making the field her retirement home. Occasionally she would check out the flowers in the Cemetery but most of the time she could be seen grazing with the horses.

Although Houdini's life had been quite carefree and relatively free from bureaucracy I guess it was inevitable that it would intervene at her passing. So when the end came some big decisions had to be made. It seems quite strange that there are now four generations of my family in Colwall Churchyard and yet in the fifty-acre field adjacent to the Cemetery it is illegal to bury one dead sheep due to some ridiculous EU regulation. This meant that poor old Houdini was destined to be thrown onto a pile of dead animals in the back of a lorry and sent to an incinerator in Devon. What a state of affairs! But, the authorities don't know it all, do they?

DO WE TAKE OUR HARVEST FOR GRANTED?

Harvest has come and gone and as I noted last month, no one has had a good one. From wheat to fruit, to the autumn livestock trade, yields are down and so are incomes. The reasons: it wasn't just the rain but the early drought, the late frost and the lack of sunlight. These are just the natural causes and it won't end there. I suspect when I come to write this column in eight or nine months time (if the editor hasn't sacked me by then) you will all be paying as much as 10 per cent more for some of your basic food. Either that, or the supermarkets will be squeezing their suppliers—the farmers—so much that there will be as much as 10 per cent fewer of us.

This year's food production statistics are quite scary. There is a shortfall of some 14 per cent in the grain harvest. The harvest total is around thirteen million tonnes with one and a half million tonnes being syphoned off for the production of bio-fuels. Not only are these figures disturbing but also I have it on good authority that one of the major supermarkets has a shortfall of a million tonnes of potatoes for its annual requirement. The problems do not stop there. Fields are now so badly waterlogged that it has become almost impossible to plant the crops for next year, leaving a serious deficit for the harvest of 2013.

As a farmer I have always had serious concerns for food production not only in this country, but in the rest of the world, and with huge quantities of grain now being used for creating energy I do wonder how long it will be before we see food queues or even rationing in this country to supply an ever-increasing population. This year, of all years, proves that harvest is *not* always fine. It takes a whole year of hard work in sometimes foul conditions with no guaranteed outcome. Loss of life is not unheard of in agriculture; the machinery is big and dangerous; animals have tempers that can kill and yet I feel that the majority of the population shows little regard for the work that goes in to producing food for the dinner table. I can understand the ignorance of the urban masses as many of them don't know any different and I wonder if they even care. But, even here in the heart of the country there seems to be a lack of understanding of the perils of food production or the precarious situation that exists on farms at this present time. Many other issues such as health and safety, the realities of farming with bovine TB, the Rural Payments Agency and the continuing weight of regulations are additional burdens affecting farming families.

I'm sorry to have got onto a bit of a soapbox about this but as readers will be aware, Old Rustic always tries to say it as he sees it.

OLD RUSTIC GETS GRUMPIER!

According to my editor, or long-suffering wife Diane, I am rapidly becoming Old Grumpy rather than Old Rustic. So, just for a change, I will only briefly mention the ongoing situation at Cummins Farm; after all there are plenty of subjects to be grumpy about without mentioning sheep or the weather!

As I have often stated in the Colwall Clock the farm appears to have become tidal but, guess what, so have the side roads in and around Colwall. Not only are they awash but they are also turning into a skating rink each time we have a freeze and the pot holes resemble craters that you would normally see in some war torn third world country.

My! How times have changed. When I was a boy Cusser Thomas would arrive on his push bike from Coddington Cross where he lived with his brother, with a shovel, a spade, a broom and a set of draining rods tied to his crossbar. He cleaned out ditches, unblocked culverts and generally kept the highway maintained. He had no mobile phone, no expensive maintenance vehicle and no mini digger. He did no risk assessment or form filling and there was definitely no supervisor, strutting about in his reflective jacket and hard hat. Cusser was an interesting character. He sported a rather bushy moustache, not unlike my own, and he obviously got his nickname from the fact that he was always swearing, though nothing beyond damn, blast or bloody, which is all pretty tame judging by today's standards.

The last time I saw the old boy he was in Flap Gate Lane by the old barn, holding court with my late father, when a diesel train went up the track. It was at the time when steamers were being phased out. Cusser pulled himself up to his full height and let out a string of expletives, as he obviously had no time for those new-fangled diesel engines! These experiences are very fresh in my memory; they were all part of my growing up in a countryside where we were surrounded by some real characters that had lived through one, if not two world wars. Their homes had no running water and no electricity but they were happy with their lot, probably because they had never known any different.

Now we have progressed into the twenty-first century. Mobile phones, mini diggers, form filling, risk assessment and supervisors strutting like peacocks are the norm. Ditches and culverts are blocked or non-existent and Torvill and Dean could perform their Bolero on the road between Cummins Farm and Lavenger Bank. When I recently reported a pothole to the Highways man he wanted to know how deep it was. Well, he couldn't have asked a better man! I thought long and hard and thought of Cusser Thomas. I said, 'Well, I am six foot three inches and I'm wearing a hat. I am now standing in the pot hole and only my —— pompom is visible!' He wasn't impressed. I wondered if he'd logged my response into his computer and I imagine that it would have challenged his spell-checker.

So, to end on a positive note, the nights are drawing out and Neil manages to get to work on his scooter without too much illumination. Yes, spring is in the air. We have started lambing, the birds are pairing up and today I saw a raven carrying twigs to his nest. But the real signs of spring for me are the winter aconites at the Glebe, lovingly tended by Ben and Sally Cooper. Ben actually rang me to let me know they were in bloom so thank you Ben and thanks too for the hangover from when we last met!

RW 2676